correspondence

Poems by Hanna Abi Akl

Correspondence

Copyright © 2021 by Hanna Abi Akl
Waterton Publishing Company

All rights reserved. No part of this book may be reproduced, stored, or transmitted by any means whether auditory, graphic, mechanical,or electronic without written permission of the author, except in the case of brief excerpts used in critical articles and reviews. Unauthorized reproduction of any part of this work is illegal and is punishable by law.

Because of the dynamic nature of the Internet, any web addresses or links contained in this book may have changed since publication and may no longer be valid. The views expressed in this work are solely those of the author and do not necessarily refl ect the views of the publisher, and the publisher hereby disclaims any responsibility for them.

ISBN 978-1-7347632-0-1

watertonpublishing.com

This book is dedicated to every one of its readers.

Foreword

It has been a strange year. Normally I don't find the need to supplement my work as I believe any work of art should be sufficient and complete on its own. But as I said, this has been a strange year. Humanity seems to be going through an important shift on many levels. And there's no telling what changes this shift will bring about or what balances it will upset. Our natural mode of existing may experience an upheaval (or to the more optimistic, a renewal), and some of our core principles may come under scrutiny.

The importance of this book goes far beyond its content. It acts as a safekeeper of core concepts I believe are detrimental to us going forward. First, the concept of producing a book is itself a necessity in this era of technological revolution. It is important to preserve the stance of books as reliable providers of quality information and knowledge. Their status as such should remain intact and undiminished.

Second, the place of poetry in our world has also been put into question. Poetry is a concept that has faced changes to cope with ever-changing times. While some might question the relevance of poetry today (just as they might question the relevance and utility of any other form of art), the matter of the fact is that poetry has never stopped being relevant. It has become increasingly important to write and share poetry as it is an important (if not the most important) marker of both literature and humankind. It has documented our existence and changes along the evolutionary chain and kept our humanity together.

Finally, I find it important to address the title of this body of work. The word Correspondence has been especially chosen because it refers to conversation and dialogue. Dialogue is another important trait of our humanity and reminds us that sharing information and knowledge is a huge part of why we have succeeded and made it this far as a species. This body of work is faithful to the spirit of dialogue: each poem is constructed as a two-ended exchange between a speaker and a listener.

For readers, I hope these poems will feel personal enough to make them take on the role of listeners and be directly involved in the dialogue.

- correspondence -

Poems

two years
1

yellow morning
3

when asked if i believed in god
5

around the world
8

unhinged
10

thursday night
11

what happens in a human heart?
13

vondelpark
14

twenty-five
15

the soul of a poet
16

the last time i cried
17

the final hour
19

trouble
20

the bite of life
21

- Hanna Abi Akl -

the shave
24

the sandman
26

the fruit of life
29

the grind
30

the fall
31

the day the world began
32

swimming seas
33

scatterings
34

silly fingers
35

the bottle
37

rooftops
38

self-love
39

strangled
40

runaway dreams
41

river that keeps on going
43

- correspondence -

perpetual motion
44

room foregone by love
46

risky business
48

red street
49

poem of grief
50

rallying call
52

poem written after a fight
53

on a tuesday morning
56

paintballs
57

pulse
59

on free verse
61

poem for egyptian girl
63

on being and nothingness
64

no company
65

near the end
67

- Hanna Abi Akl -

new age
70

massacre
71

litany
73

existence
74

miraculous
75

mourning
76

love at 7 degrees
77

meditation
78

lottery ticket
79

mind over matter
80

line break
81

little dark blob
82

limits
83

je te veux
84

letter to self
86

- correspondence -

geometry
87

genesis
88

if she likes it
90

insomnia
91

i have a problem
92

Honesty
94

euphoria
95

going home
96

corridor
97

empty faces on a beautiful spring day
99

empty fillings
101

correspondence
103

do all creatures love equally?
104

deconstruction
106

clenched speech
107

the seal
108

closing remarks
109

barricades
110

carnal notebook
111

beirut
113

cherry tree season
118

At gravekeeper's request
120

art & science
122

anatomy of the human race
123

absence
124

a plausible death
125

a singular life running its course
127

alone on a spring day
129

a certain loneliness
132

a good man
133

- correspondence -

untold legend
135

a sad day in paris
136

- correspondence -

two years

let your cigarette hand
sparkle in the twinkling night
sky as your favorite
composer comes to life

and i sit naked in bed
waiting for you to crawl in
my arms and burrow your head
in my chest searching
for elusive things
i am yet to understand

the neighbors next door
are fighting and i wonder
how can two people make love
while two others fight?

maybe the night air
we've been inhaling
all this time is different

- Hanna Abi Akl -

and maybe i am not meant
to think about things
beyond simple pleasures.

- correspondence -

yellow morning

like others i have a
crippling fear of death
it is the only
subject where words do little
to comfort me

i fear as much the long, slow
suffering as the
thunderous, sudden
end and i believe
even if my body could
somehow escape it
my mind surely won't

this attachment to life is
a sickness i pray
is long-lasting

and as long as it does not
spiral out of its course and
become terminal

- Hanna Abi Akl -

i should be able
to safely make it.

- correspondence -

when asked if i believed in god

i said how could i with you
right here looking at
me with the sadness
of a martyr who
died without a cause
a martyr betrayed by fate
not by death itself
but the manner of dying

how could i when your eyes gaze
beyond the ceiling
and swallow space and
swallow galaxies
and swallow the universe

how could i when you recite
verses from holy scriptures
about meaning until
meaning is lost and

- Hanna Abi Akl -

trivial and burdened with
incredible weight
it implodes the next morning
next to a burnt-out
cigarette bum in
the paper ashtray we
set on the bed stand

how could i when i worshipped
such sacred things as
syllables and words
and books and numbers
and mystical equations

when very few of
us — the best maybe —
can barely hope for
a crossover or
a passage of rites
or a pass to the
eternal kingdom

while others like myself are

- correspondence -

busy catering for this
small world; these windows you see;
these wooden floor panels
layered with crumbs you walk on

those are the ones trying to
settle whatever
scores they have left to
leave this place debt-free.

- Hanna Abi Akl -

around the world

make room for the sun
blasting on the bed sheets where
wine-stained portions left
their mark not too long ago

hop on a subway train at
midnight; get off at
a random station;
throw your phone in the gutter;
and ask no questions:

this is the way to
put the world at ease.

befriend a stray cat
watch him walk behind
you and frolic to
the glimmering of your keys

go home and take off your shoes
and your socks and your pants and

- correspondence -

pour yourself a drink
if you drink and if
you don't then turn off the news
and those eyes beating
senselessly against
the skull with no mind
that slipped and rolled over the
hillside to the great
avenue dark-lit by
torches where only
strangers know the way. there is
no way out of this mad life
except halting the mad days
turning sad and grim and
blue and pale and white.

retreat: man is alive when
he kicks back at everything
and allows himself to sit
quietly in the shade and
watch a tree branch sway
in the gentle breeze.

– Hanna Abi Akl –

unhinged

like a white paper
with no chance shredded into
bits; some days caught between
clamping
down on words that won't give in

or drawn by the illusion
of a ballistic mind that
spews prophecies on paper

the same mind that taunts
the blue wave knowing
it will live its final days
in unrest before it hits

wondering what remains when
all traces of existence
are washed away?

- correspondence -

thursday night

it's the last sip of whiskey
dropping like a
rolling thundercloud

it's a stack of unanswered
letters slid under the door

it's a girl drinking red wine
in pink shorts smiling
across the hardwood

it's the battle against the
gamble of whitman
drawing the last line
the last leaf of grass

it's death stalking you
at the street corner

it's the cry of corpses in

- Hanna Abi Akl -

venice, in lombardy
riding in military
vehicles to nowhere sea

it's the asphalt still fresh
with footprints and blood

it's the deranged agony
of the ones that try
to live with themselves.

- correspondence -

what happens in a human heart?

carve it open and you won't
find any instructions;
just a misleading
path every step of the way

you abandon yourself
in a cavity of pain
a butterfly in
a hurricane: vital,
fragile and obscene

finally it becomes the
estranged lover you
never find waiting for you

yet you still wake up
every day hoping you will.

– Hanna Abi Akl –

vondelpark

in late afternoons
we liked to hide in the park
under the black alder trees
and smoke our cigarettes
watching the sky sink
into point blank

& when night came
for us like a deathmark
ominously gliding
over our shadows
we knew we were the greatest
lovers in an unfit &
blasphemous universe.

- correspondence -

twenty-five

rode the subway train

ordered a croissant

walked into the specter of
a city with a handful
of dreams and a bucket full
of promises

spoke in a foreign
tongue in a small antique shop

slept on the floor boards with no
bed and the uncertainty
of tomorrow

looked at you with the
eyes of love for the first time

and life was not what it was —
life was not a selfish dream.

– Hanna Abi Akl –

the soul of a poet

teach me to grasp love
like one of your stubborn boys
full of bravado and
boiling defiance

i yearn for a rebirth
a second coming
as a gentler soul

teach me to slip between your
fingertips as you
caress my skin;
to hum at the sight
of a hummingbird

carry me out of
these dark faithless woods

there is only one
way to ruin a life:
to take the love out of it.

- correspondence -

the last time i cried

i was 13 and alone
at the graveyard staring at
my father's grave the
day after the funeral
and death was leering at me

peeling layers of
tears i was proud to
cry with nobody watching

especially my mother
whose face blessed with pride said
her little boy did not cry

and i was lucky enough
to know those were the last tears
and they would dry out
forever after this day

and i would no longer cry
and live by my mother's words

- Hanna Abi Akl -

and i have been right
ever since that day.

- correspondence -

the final hour

a death bed is not
the last thing that stands
between you and death ⌧

a death bed is answering
the question of existence
with suicide;

it is the sickness
of love and life;

it is relinquishing
talent and dreams;

some have already prepared
for it long before their time.

– Hanna Abi Akl –

trouble

these are times when even young
bodies suddenly turn old

each one like a candlestick
waiting to burn:
very few of it
remains properly intact.

- correspondence -

the bite of life

many years ago
i was a kid pale and weak

now i am a kid
whose frustrated soul
is ready to burst

who knows things might end
just as they began

and the sky is a
huge cloud taking shape
and i am a hitchhiker
to no man's land
somewhere untarnished
by the human hand
and un-coveted
by savage eyes

wishing to sit down
by a stream and let

- Hanna Abi Akl -

the kid out for some air
let him breathe the fresh
air of bliss that dogs
breathe and bark about
and lie down on the green grass
and stare at the part of sky
that still looks like sky

and remember that
werewolves and
gargoyles and dragons
are just made-up things
— or maybe not —
but far from this place

and feel the roots grow
under my feet and
think of the reaper
chasing me all my life
threatening to come for me
in my sleep or worse ⌑
in waking moment

- correspondence -

and i would kick him out;
there aren't many things
worth living for but
some wholehearted
experiences just fill
you up and make you
think of sweet jam and
creamy buttered mornings
when everything is awake
and death has no upper hand.

- Hanna Abi Akl -

the shave

at 17 i had a
chin full of hair stubs
that cast a light shade of beard;
i walked — a man among boys
who looked on sick with envy

i tried shaving for
the first time at home:
i took the cream in one hand
the razor in the other
i stood in front of
the mirror and thought
"this should be easy"

i cut my lower lip and
trembled as the blood came out
to the harrowing cries of
my wailing mother

poor wailing mama
who cried knowing she couldn't

- correspondence -

turn me to a man

and i cried knowing
the answer was becoming
a man on my own

well papa, i don't
know where you are but
i'm doing better
with the damn razor.

— Hanna Abi Akl —

the sandman

these four walls are not your home
this country is not your home

make the river cry
slam every door every way

reach for the sun with
a roar of your voice

to purge every island and
put out every forest fire

make the beam of life your thread
and tread lightly

look out for demons
big red-eyed monsters
lurking in the shadows with
big hairy fiendish
hands; unclipped fingers;

- correspondence -

dump the scriptures and
go back to splashing
in puddles of faith
hope was never real
it was just lettered
on banners now taken down
from every store front

the bikers, greasy
repairmen will drop
their tools and machinery
and follow — lead the
way: make carrots sprout,
gingerbread houses appear
as you hop along

don't forget the music as
you go: rock, jazz, classical

now wait. stop. don't forget to
taste bread hot from the oven
searing like the flesh
after a good tan in the

- Hanna Abi Akl -

noon sun in golden daylight

track back. go home wherever
that may be curl up
inside a tent or
sleep soundly on your
1-bedroom apartment floor

the sandman waits solemnly
for your eyes to shut
like the last door shut
behind you as you
enter and plot for
tomorrow in your slumber.

- correspondence -

the fruit of life

right between your legs:
a small bud of hair
an aromatic scent and
a glistening mouth
that opens at the
touch of my fingers.

- Hanna Abi Akl -

the grind

a poetess threatens to
quit and throw all her
work up in the air

every poem she
ever wrote slashed;
lines smashed into the
ground and scattered like marbles

an ominous death
hits when yet another bright
apprentice loses her flame.

- correspondence -

the fall

i think of those who braved it
and took the chance and
made the jump and pierced
the final surface

i have imagined
in fierce dreams what lies
on the other end

but i am not like
them: i am not brave

unlike them — i'm not ready.

— Hanna Abi Akl —

the day the world began

fear like a torch is enough
to drive some of us
out of houses, gardens deep
into the woods of the world
probing like fearful
wanderers wanting
only to be felt
and understood

leaving others in
a standstill, engulfed,
consumed until finally
relinquishing and
accepting it entirely

i am of the latter kind:
i haven't moved since the day
the world began for me.

- correspondence -

swimming seas

pushing my fingers
one last time through your thick
dark
hair i wonder how many
seas it would have taken me
to salvage you in my arms.

− Hanna Abi Akl −

scatterings

i offer you god
whose ubiquitous presence
you will not take lightly in
hazardous moments
or chance encounters:
that is where he appears

otherwise everything is
governed by laws so
intricately knit they form
the portrait of existence

there is room for each of us:
we are marked like ink dots on
this canvas that will
remember us forever.

- correspondence -

silly fingers

silly fingers that
can barely string two
sentences together
silly fingers that
can barely push the button
to offset the world's demise
silly fingers that
can barely return
the caress of a
faithful woman

they are worn out, dirty and
hardened by trial and time
playing catch-up with
this degenerating mind

how will it survive without
them especially when the
lips have failed time and again
scrambling for parts of speech?

- Hanna Abi Akl -

these fingers will defy the
laws of time; they will defy
the gauntlet thrown at them and
punch like a fighter
little fingers — bearers of
what's left of this heart
graceful actors of my will
don't forsake this mind

the same way the rest
of this body will.

– correspondence –

the bottle

i just want to hug it tight
like a warm blanket
and escape from my
sober state into
drunk euphoria

and hope to hold it this close
like a friend in need
when the last flame consumes me
and i'm fingered by the dark.

— Hanna Abi Akl —

rooftops

i look outside and
the fog is lifted
and the raven sky returns
descending like a shadow
on these parisian rooftops

i am blessed with grief
and blessed with sorrow
and with the gift of living.

- correspondence -

self-love

an affectionate
smile can make my knees buckle
and soften my heart

despite this glaring
weakness i preach self-love like
a religion — and i'm both
its most ardent believer
and heretic.

strangled

words make life
out of this hashed entity

critics will rise and drop dead
like crickets on summer nights
and i will make the wind blow
my way until my breath runs
out and i'll save the limelight
for another life

in this one i'll just leave drops
for them to pick up
and scoff at as much as they
please after i'm gone.

- correspondence -

runaway dreams

quitting the act of
love was like quitting
smoking, you taught me,
and spent the remaining days
smoking more and loving less

but i refuse to believe
hours spent outside
on the porch exiled
from the human world
under the glistening sun
were mere fabled dreams
our little hearts latched
onto desperately

i like to believe in a
forbidden eternity
where such sacred dreams
run to — it is a closed door
with a small hole that
the light reaches and seeps through

- Hanna Abi Akl -

one we cannot watch over
or constantly guard

one we cannot touch
let alone open.

- correspondence -

river that keeps on going

i drink my coffee
cold; somewhere a river keeps
going through the countryside
past the windmills, past
the striking of clocks

somewhere a river keeps on
going past the flow of time
past the spark of the
insane galaxies

i ask her how i can make
my name sound less foreign at
poetry readings
she shrugs and replies: you can't

and i gather few poems
a short selection
to be read to attentive
scholars looking for answers:
they will not find them.

- Hanna Abi Akl -

perpetual motion

she walks on tiptoes
no ⌧ she tip-toes from
the bathroom to the kitchen
to the music of Piaf

as i sit in my corner
with Tom Waits hooked to my ears
and wait for her to ask me
what i'd like to eat.

her floating feet remind me
of first spring: green tapestry;
an exploding cosmos of
petals twinkling down on me;
the earthy taste of fertile
land baked beneath my two feet

i see it all: crawling dawn
across our fettered bodies
eyes doused with her sky blue toes

- correspondence -

and reply to her
like a shy little
boy talking up his
dear mother: make those
eggs you like so much.

- Hanna Abi Akl -

room foregone by love

torn books, paintings smashed
into fragments of broken
eternity

old letters perfumed with love

songs we started and
never finished

keychains that held us
together like the
knot of destiny

like helpless fish flopping on
dry land the smoke clouds
of our faces growing in
the blue flame condensed into
a column of fire

i too believe we
are back to burning

- correspondence -

and drowning in the
mist of the moment

i too believe in a pale
dotted tomorrow
that refuses to
give itself
to either of us.

– Hanna Abi Akl –

risky business

crowds are not interesting:
no more than a distraction
they always gather in the
obvious and dull places

the best places aren't easy
to see; instead of
following light one
must follow silence

that's what leads to the
most charming venues.

- correspondence -

red street

it's a small street on the west
side of town where i used to
hide during my college years

red street was always best with
its red cafe that
served coffee with cinnamon
sticks, its one-way street
with no space to park,
its drunks and hookers
and smokers and thieves

who taught me best what
i needed to learn.

- Hanna Abi Akl -

poem of grief

i've fallen into a world
of unbounded cruelty

where the past matters
so little and survival
is the sole mantra

is existing enough? or
are we championed by
this accomplishment
of being borne into a
planet that seldom
opens its arms and
reluctantly welcomes us
in its hostile dystopia?

the wastelands we call
graves tell us our fates are sealed

which is reason enough for
us to give up our

- correspondence -

darkest secrets for
a little more breathing space.

- Hanna Abi Akl -

rallying call

nobody knows what kind of
bug's bitten us but
centuries later
we are still fighting
for the same causes:
peace, justice, equality

now it's more killing
and the only thing
anyone wants to hold on
to is their own life

another century and
there'll be only
a handful of us
saying what millions
are saying today

and maybe give up
their lives to say it.

– correspondence –

poem written after a fight

our worst days are like
hot summers the air
thick with regret trying to
penetrate our lungs like sand

they're like icy nights
of respite that make
me wish for your words

normally i hide in you
i cut open a
line between your breasts
and conceal myself
when everything turns
dark and the last ray
of light is eclipsed

and to think a flick of your
finger on the back

— Hanna Abi Akl —

of my ear lobe would suffice

take me not in hiding i'm
a blasphemous saint
sentenced for the cross
on any good day
i am a faithless
kid standing in his
mother's kitchen to the sound
of church choir singing

i have sent bones of the dead
rattling, packing to the crypt
watched them lowered to the grave

but it's better to be dead
than detached ▢ we can't be both
the heart can't bear it

to say i have no words for
you is untrue: i have the
words they come down on me like
a holy litany and

- correspondence -

vanish completely

o! your flick on my ear lobe!
to repent in your bosom!

- Hanna Abi Akl -

on a tuesday morning

brewing my coffee
i await the moment your
eyes make first contact
with the world.

- correspondence -

paintballs

i feel my mind slipping here
in this dark doldrum
digging its own grave
and then looting it

it is a common feeling
of slumping, sliding
into dark slumber

black visions engulf
innards of my brain
shredding piece by piece
leaving it in shards

i always wanted to paint
i believe it is freedom
but starting for the first time
is like re-writing ▢
your fear of ruining
it keeps you away

- Hanna Abi Akl -

i tell those in my circle
i would like to paint
i will pick it up
knowing well enough
the day i pick up the brush
and stare at the white canvas
will cause the same scare
as staring down at the page

knowing i will start
is solace enough
for now, but someday
maybe writing won't cut it
anymore (won't sustain me)
won't push back the dark

come that time, where will i run?

- correspondence -

pulse

here we are: half-clothed
the afternoon in
shards among unfinished beer
bottles and snack bowls
and minds hypnotized
by unending tv shows

the house is damp the
curtains colorless
the furniture pale

your hand in my hand
you feel my pulse for
the first time like a
drum beat vibrating
across the floor boards

no sign of beauty
to unearth from this
room only decaying lives
bodies that have surrendered

- Hanna Abi Akl -

and caved - growing old
hand in hand with time

but us being here
alone together
hacked and undone by
the mundanity of days

your hand in my hand
i swear: we are beautiful.

- correspondence -

on free verse

it's the new norm for
every poet on the bloc:
free from pretension

it certainly has appeal:
breaking away from
rigid form, rhythm, rhyme

being more loose, it
is unburdened, free:
a buffer for expression

but where is the line
that keeps this art form
from becoming erratic?

liberating verse
renders it vulnerable:
breakable like glass

without form, it has no frame

- Hanna Abi Akl -

badly conceived, it shatters
whereas this one doesn't.

- correspondence -

poem for egyptian girl

her dark frizzy hair and her
glasses evaporated

the note she left read:
i tried to survive, and failed

rainbow girl, ride into the
rainbow sky and let
the pyramids adorn you
with the purest light.

on being and nothingness

in our undying quest to
free ourselves from true
and complete loneliness through
love we find that the
one person that should
understand us when
no one else does is
sometimes the person
that understands us the least.

- correspondence -

no company

i think of your eyes
the eyes of an enchantress
the eyes of a mother that
lulls her cub to sleep

the eyes of a smoker that
chases strangers from
street to street begging
for a single cigarette

the eyes that watch over a
sacred valley of oak trees
as the albatross takes its
long awaited flight
and do not close till it lands

the eyes that utter the words
good night even when the night
is long and restless

the eyes that latch on

- Hanna Abi Akl -

even when the body is
inebriated

the eyes that look down
and beg for absolution
from the bloody cross

they are enough to
soften any dream.

- correspondence -

near the end

loose hand working at
this table, crooked glasses,
dim lighting, crackling floor boards

i am the epitome
of uncertainty:
formidable doubt
and antagonism
in the face of creation

moving farther and
farther away from
the creator and
his ultimate wrath
pushing me harder
toward a bottomless pit

i have stared into
the abyss and have
seen nothing but empty words
and lashing out after poor

- Hanna Abi Akl -

days and poorer years

days when you pour cold water
on your defunct soul
to wash away the
filth and stink of time

and attempt to forget and
attempt to flee how
could i when this hand
is crippled and frail
and the flesh itches
and asks mercifully to
be stretched and ripped out
cold from the body?

too many nights have passed since
my hands caught fire with words

the only thing that still lives
willingly in this place is
the typewriter music box
playing the same tune

- correspondence -

reminding me how
fast an artist can grow stale.

- Hanna Abi Akl -

new age

make this feeble heart
fly — take it away
now that it's a nameless thing
i've harbored and lost

today it's reduced
to nothing, stripped of essence

and love — that heavy
chest secretly sleeping for
so long now opened, tarnished,
worthless makes all else
look ordinary.

where are we going
alone and is it
still worth getting there?

- correspondence -

massacre

deserted city
with open parks and playgrounds
but no children to play in

the dead wailing of sirens
flashing in and out of streets
before dying like the first
flower in autumn ⌧

rich incense exhumes temples
abandoned by the pious:
the faithful no longer stand

hospital doors are open
their floors, walls, ceilings pale
white
gusts blow through them like
sand desert heat waves

no choirs, no carolers, the
holiday songs forgotten

- Hanna Abi Akl -

replaced by skeletal shots
of dumb leaders who
perished at the city gates
dragged back to the scene
the last food market,
tavern, bar, cafe
open for business
serving poltergeists
that forgot to die

there has been talk of
erasing this place
from the history of man
zapping its existence and
tragic end from memory

a nation shot to the ground
its people decimated
but we don't know what killed them.

- correspondence -

litany

a
person
is
a
sentence
once uttered
can't
be
unsaid.

existence

if the rich can find their way
then the poor can cling to me
i will be their wings
and — once clipped — we will
ride together through
the desert like sand
snakes or desert ants

right until we fall
into the pit and
the holy hand catches us

fists silently parading
what's left of our faith
to guide our actions

none daring to ask:
who wishes for salvation
or the golden gates
of eternity?

- correspondence -

miraculous

now this miracle
of a woman rests
beside me ⸺ we've spent
countless nights spitting half-
mashed
words at each other

and not once have i told her
how still my heart becomes when
her eyes close and fall
into a deep sleep

at the present time
of writing that is
the only thing worth saying.

mourning

love is a mirage
waiting to be filled

and when it can't be filled it
becomes a shadow
without a purpose

how can you love me
when my touch is like
ice so cold it burns?

you are a magnificent
rhapsody destined for the
skies of the acropolis

but you'll always be
an unfinished love letter
that falls a syllable short

or arrives too late.

- correspondence -

love at 7 degrees

how can you say i
don't love you enough?
is my love measurable?

i am no sentient being
but i believe it isn't too
hard to love: all it
takes is forgiveness

maybe that's the part
everyone has trouble with

you say i don't love
you enough. i say i do.

you say you don't love
me enough. i say you do.

you say, what now? nothing, i
say. let's drink more coffee and
listen to the rain.

meditation

i look blaringly into
the night: it stares blankly back
at me — asking me questions
of eternity,
faith i left behind
and lost innocence.

- correspondence -

lottery ticket

if i wake up one morning
with the terrible urge to
give it all up and get rich

does that mean i lost
or i've given up?

- Hanna Abi Akl -

mind over matter

behind every face
there are corridors
to a great looming
silence

a willful innate
shadow that gently
runs its fingertips
along the scalp of the self

sometimes safeguarding
something purposeful

and at others something that
barely knows it's there.

- correspondence -

line break

    we imitate birds:
    your chirping a line of verse
    and mine ⌑ a line break.

– Hanna Abi Akl –

little dark blob

i've missed you like the
pages i will never write

i've missed you like this little
dark blob i am afraid to
touch but still long for

i've missed you like the self i
know i will never become

the one that shreds itself for
others; that lives in
its own spiritual realm

that itches for a little
peace in a room with
some sunlight and a
piano by the window.

- correspondence -

limits

glasses hang upside-down from
the ceiling as the liquor
pours into my throat

i've spent innumerable
days looking for mystical
answers to the world's
most bizarre questions

and in the process i've drowned
into unspeakable depths.

je te veux

when you came to me
in small steps that night
in some strange parking lot love
invited itself
and took away the
instruments of my sorrow

i was no longer afraid
of growing old and alone

my only lasting fear was
death but even that became
bearable with you

and you told me i looked like
a mean machine i looked like
your father in disguise but
behind my disfigured self
behind my treacherous looks
there was a certain frailty
that you tapped into

- correspondence -

and all the elements burned
and every city became
a spherical dream
we could alter as we pleased
and my words had meaning and
your breath thrust into my chest
made cold winters a
short-lived affair ⬚ yes:

this is the way spring
arrived at our door.

- Hanna Abi Akl -

letter to self

i am layers and
layers of unrest rolling
in gravel to silence the
tremor in these ailing bones

head deep underground
i wonder what is
this crucial thing worth
fighting for at the surface?

- correspondence -

geometry

society is
a circle and politics
is the square inscribed in it

and those who have decided
to preserve what's left of their
identity are cutouts

do you get it now?

- Hanna Abi Akl -

genesis

the heart breaks for a city
the city breaks for
its people, its sweepers, its
cleaners, its cargo workers

show me the heart that
doesn't break; doesn't hug the
oldest building as
it shatters and disappears

show me the city
that does not mourn its fallen
whose pillars embrace
white coffins and freeze
time and distort space

show me the people
that pray without words
their lips cold, white, tasting ash
holding debris in their hands
and burned family pictures

- correspondence -

show me the stone whereupon
civilizations are built —
i too would like to
rest upon it long
enough to turn it
into a city.

- Hanna Abi Akl -

if she likes it

she's demystified
every secret, every fear

and poked through every
crack in this glass case

honey, you can break
me all you want just
not all at once, please

do it piece by piece.

- correspondence -

insomnia

i am neither asleep nor
awake; i am in
a semi-state hanging by
a thread at both ends.

- Hanna Abi Akl -

i have a problem

she says,
you are selfish, arrogant
and a pretentious liar

okay, i say and
avoid eye-contact
and a possible conflict

i flip through a poetry
magazine: just a bunch of
nobodies like me

what will be left of
me after i exit this
world through the holy wormhole?

and what will be left
of this furious woman
standing in front of me in
pure rage after i
decide to leave her?

- correspondence -

a little more than
her perfume that smells
like oven-made potatoes
i hope.

- Hanna Abi Akl -

Honesty

first traverse the labyrinth
of your soul; only
then can you reveal yourself.

- correspondence -

euphoria

watching you walk along the
sandy beach in your
white bikini dotted with
sky-blue flowers and dipping
your pink toes in the
cold atlantic waters can
cure a man and stir
emotions where there were none.

going home

you made me promise
that we would visit
every garden; sit
on every wet bench
our clothes soaking in
the leftover rain

roam weightlessly from one place
to another undisturbed
underneath the warm
sun until we learn
to smell home again.

- correspondence -

corridor

straight from my childhood
like a pulse from yesterday
it was there that ghosts
and other darkly things lived

i can still picture my room
and that corridor
but never the end of it

each night i thought of
the courage my parents had
to muster to go in there
how unfair it was
for them to come face to face
with that corridor
while i hid in my safe room

when i don't know where to go
i think of that corridor
and wish i had the courage
of my parents to traverse

- Hanna Abi Akl -

it'll take that dark route
all the way and maybe find
some light at the end.

– correspondence –

empty faces on a beautiful spring day

what wonders i have
seen in nature ▢ and
what sorrows i've learned from it

eventually
the mortal heart loosens and
dies much earlier than the
brain or any body part

yet some continue past this
death like hollow entities

they walk among us

they are constant reminders
to the rest carrying a
figment of the memory
of what once was or
could have been full ▢ but

- Hanna Abi Akl -

chose to be empty.

- correspondence -

empty fillings

deep in the hallways
of a childhood i disowned
i was always at
the margin of everything

i've built my way into life
with cautious optimism and
trusting that i'll see good come
out of people but
with measured precaution so
that if it ever comes down
to cutting the rope
my hand'll be ready

it's hard to project
a lifetime where the walls are
your only friends with
no liaison with no
attachments with no one to
run to when darkness eats up
what's left of your world

- Hanna Abi Akl -

maybe it's easier to
not think about it
to avoid building
the idea so much it
becomes real, so much it
becomes obsession,
so much it becomes
a lifelong pursuit

can you hear them? these empty
fillings clamoring
for a taste of love?

correspondence

my dear, this world is
circumstantial by nature
and so were we at first — but
we have turned circumstance to
habit and habit
to norm and norm to
fate and fate to poetry.

— Hanna Abi Akl —

do all creatures love equally?

i would wake up one
morning in love with
a woman and fall
in love with another one
on my way to work

maybe my failings in love
are not my own and the fault
is in those that learned
to love better than i did

i've never held anyone
in my arms and thought:
you are mine for life

that sentence resonates in
my mind like little
shards of broken glass

- correspondence -

love is like a door
held ajar for me: i can
get in and out fast enough
but in the end i always
find myself on the outside

if love were a city i
would live on its outskirts and
gaze at its gorgeous buildings
shining in the sun

only i would not
dare inhabit it.

– Hanna Abi Akl –

deconstruction

is god a stick man?
is god present in
my deepest concavities?

is god the almighty whale
slumbering at the bottom
of the deepest ocean? or
is he the sunken
submarine made relevant
by the few divers
who visit it and
poke at it every once in
a thousand tides?

- correspondence -

clenched speech

what i put down here
is my only form
of communing with myself

just as i could not reveal
to the ordinary soul
the gripping insomnia that
keeps me up at night
or the terrible fear that
startles me awake
every morning or
the tantrums i grapple with
in my conscious state

i'm only able
to put down here whatever
it is i'm unable to
say — and that is both
my greatest weakness and strength.

the seal

crows gather on a
branch above my head
their luminescent eyes dark
orbs that fill the night
there's eternity
in their gaze; there's the
promise of sorrow; there's the
mirror of a loveless life

i hereby beg all powers
to join forces and save me
from this cruel fate.

- correspondence -

closing remarks

and so we part: you go your
way and i go mine

until we meet again i
will keep the part of
you i wrote about

the part that makes sense to me
the part that is now
immortal in these pages

the part that seems to
be about enough for now.

barricades

what sick melancholy is
toying with my fate?
i feel like a puppet on
a string being played
by a puppeteer

except i'm at this
point where i no longer care
about performing.

- correspondence -

carnal notebook

crazy days: little drops of
nostalgia drooping through the
faucets of my brain
i remember growing up
in a good home; how
they kept feeding me
the philosophy
of the working man
(out of love and concern for
my well-being, my
mother used to say)

now i'm a working-man and
there's hardly any work out
there for me; i'm always one
step behind the rest of the
world; instead of touching on
to something new i'm back to
square one, slumping through the
hours
under the hard sun for an

- Hanna Abi Akl -

hour's worth at night alone with
my feet up, soul soaked like a
wet sponge ready to release
the few words that come.
they are my joy.

- correspondence -

beirut

no, don't do this to me; i've
traded your smoke-infested
sewer-smelling street
capital for spring-filled views

why do you keep popping up
from tiny holes in my head
after you've frozen me out?

what stops you from evolving
and why do you resist it
so much? instead of holding
the club i've given you and
hitting back you've gone
and ejected me
from your precious soil

and now i'm the stranger forced
to wander for a new home
a new way of life

- Hanna Abi Akl -

you're at a standstill
be careful: my words won't yield
to the dangers that
threaten you but my
gut says you just might

you don't relent enough that's
your problem; you're not
aggressive and tenacious
you only built me
to be that way — but
it's your weakness that drove me
out; i have to grow and i
cannot find growth in your bud

beirut do you like fire?
do you like the screams of a
million souls burning in hell?

your pillars are slabs of wood
waiting to crumble
and i have seen what's out there
out there's a moving wheel while

- correspondence -

you are a flat tire

why can't i speak your language?
why can't i listen to your
music? why can't i recite
the verses of your poets?

i look like a yellow child
of the sun dumped into this
world walking towards
the crusade of myself that
starts at your feet and
ends maybe in the next world

whatever i pass by in
between is ephemeral
and only serves as
an imprint in my
ever-expanding soul that
you can no longer contain

i've been your child for long and
i've hid in your shadows and

- Hanna Abi Akl -

suffered when you suffered and
bled when you got bloodied and
crawled when you fell but now i
am standing tall — why must you
weep? why must you fail?

like the other children i've
been released into the wild
and now i walk with
aspirations between my
fingers tickling the
rays of the sun while
you still try to grow a tree
where your cedars once stood tall

it shouldn't be this way
and some worlds deserve better
and you are a part of that
but you've neglected
every warning sign
and you refuse to listen
and now your city burns and
your people burn and their eyes

- correspondence -

drown in tears and flames
and my poor mother and my
nameless friends that are
no longer in my spirit
except in letters they send
i hang on my walls

let me bash my skull one more
time and pretend things were not
this way — do i have
to re-write the churches and
the scripts of humanity
for you to get better or
occupy a better place
in this life? i can't.

i can barely write;
now give yourself in pieces
to the wind and let
me remember you the way
i like while i sing your name.

— Hanna Abi Akl —

cherry tree season

we missed it this year
in that big french park

i remember this time last
year how things were free: the wind
galloping outside, the trees
waltzing, performing
in a spectacle

we were free to speak
free to sing and dance

and now that's all washed
up and she says she
is constricted and
she can barely walk
around me without
irritating me

yes, it's true and i'm still a
naive man who thinks

- correspondence -

a moment like watching the
cherry trees blossom can fix
everything and stitch
us back together

but last night i communed with
the crickets outside on the
porch and they told me to leave
my love for her at the door
and put out the fight in me

it's bad enough i
have to tell her i
have neither the courage nor
the heart to carry
on — but to have to
explain that we won't
be seeing the trees?

- Hanna Abi Akl -

At gravekeeper's request

there is something crucial to
be done here, something
to be decided

and that's what we choose
to take with us to the grave

it won't be scented towels
or spiritual ramblings;
it won't be the next-
door-neighbor's tweety bird whose
morning songs you liked

it won't be the moon
even if you asked for it

when i heed the final call
i will carry none of that
none of me and none of you

save for the righteousness in

- correspondence -

your voice when you say my name.

- Hanna Abi Akl -

art & science

my fascination
for language has gone
far beyond scientific
curiosity:

it is a device
that has altered my
soul and allowed it
the freedom to roam
in and out of this
world as it pleases.

- correspondence -

anatomy of the human race

so much has been made of what
little is understood of
our world; and so little is
made of how much there
is yet to uncover and
comprehend: we are

the breed of the genius,
the mad, the brave, the washed-up
the doomed — totaled and
reclusive; ever-
retreating into
our prisoned selves when
our collective life alone
tells us of our flaws
and failures as a species.

- Hanna Abi Akl -

absence

sometimes strikes like a
bat slicing through the dark with
its wings cunning and weightless

this terrible void staring
from the closet between the
clothes slowly sucking
at everything like
a vacuum; whispers that a
voice could restore order as
you reach for the sparrow and
the butterfly — knowing that
they will not save you.

- correspondence -

a plausible death

woke up to the smell of death
and rot in my coffee cup

i feel the world slipping from
my fingers through hollow eyes

my muse is absent and my
days are already condemned
before they begin: i walk
through endless revolving doors
spinning perpetually
between a life that is here
and somewhere else; if i could
take it all back and begin
again; send the fish
back to the deep end

reset the motion
of the earth and the
tides and the currents

- Hanna Abi Akl -

maybe rebirth is
the only answer
for failure; maybe bringing
back yesterday will force the
muse out of her hiding in-
to the arms of tomorrow.

- correspondence -

a singular life running its course

a murky evening livid
with pointless human
howls; sometimes i dream
of being haunted
by loneliness like
an empty prison

you phone and ask: what
is prison to you?

it's being away
from you; it's being
away from somebody; it's
being consumed by
somebody long enough to
detach from yourself

it's a singular
light bulb in the midst

- Hanna Abi Akl -

of this frigid air

i haven't the force
to change it nor the
will: what's the use when i know
the next one will burn
until it can no longer
emit any light

and don't we all just
burn until we stop

and we no longer
feel this piercing cold?

in every adversity
we overcome we
set ourselves up for
the most glorious defeat.

- correspondence -

alone on a spring day

ashamed to be a
sentimentalist
in an era where
the human heart is strained by
ego, jealousy and hate

i feel more connection with
this machine here — it
is reliable
and loyal to me
and bends to my will at ease
without fuss or fight

look up any human on
the street and you can see from
his eyes that he is ready
to pick a fight but i'm still
fond of them strangely

i still like to see
them gather out in

- Hanna Abi Akl -

the open; the sun shining;
walking their dogs; conversing
from windows and balconies

it's a warm feeling
that solitude robs you from
for security

even thinking of
rose-water lilies
tight, clenching, steadfast
in their little ponds

thinking of evading for
a while just to get
away from this race

what good will it do?

man is social — that
is his greatest weakness — one
from which he can't recover

- correspondence -

lock him up for a day and
his eyes start to burn
and his skin itches
and his toes curl up
and his knees buckle

now outside an orange tree
perched in the quiet
night extends its branch
to me heavy with
fruit ripe and juicy

i wonder if i should grab
one — and maybe another
for my next-door neighbor.

- Hanna Abi Akl -

a certain loneliness

i last left my sorrow on
a night stand next to
an unmade bed; tonight i
return to make the
bed and find that it
is no longer there.

- correspondence -

a good man

my father died a good man.
that's the version of
him that i was taught.

in 13 short years
i remember so
little of him, his
words, his actions. for the best
part of my memory he
remains largely unknown. i
guess that's the way he
wanted it: to live
his life quiet and unknown.

it hardly helps with dying:
we do not escape death or
the manner in which we die
there's simply no controlling
it or tweaking it

it will happen to us all

- Hanna Abi Akl -

and when it does the best thing
to do is to be as best
prepared as we can

it won't deface death
nor alleviate it

but father, in that
last moment lying there on
your deathbed, waiting for the
great and terrible reaper

i believe a lot
of good shone from you.

- correspondence -

untold legend

please understand me:
when the time comes for my world
to fall apart i will push
away those closest to me
to save them from this descent

and do remember:
i have bathed in rivers of
darkness and lived in
houses fit for death
at the edge of life

only to forge a path most
of you are still looking for.

- Hanna Abi Akl -

a sad day in paris

i turn on the tv and
remember the world
is still in riots

that strangely feel like
they are happening
in my back alley

i turn off the tv, chew
the last bite off a 3-day
old baguette turned stiff

and patiently wait
for the final uprising
to roll back the centuries.